Words of Fucking Wisdom
A Journal for

the Spirited Soul II

MIMI MARGARITA

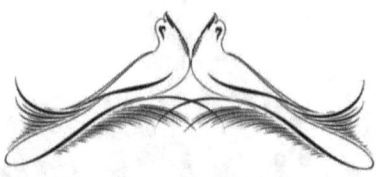

This journal belongs to:

THERE'S ALWAYS ANOTHER OPPORTUNITY TO CARRY ON AND BE FUCKING AWESOME!

PUBLISHED BY WINDSURF PUBLISHING LLC
GREENWICH, CT
COPYRIGHT © 2023 WINDSURF PUBLISHING LLC
ISBN: 978-1-936509-33-1

ALL RIGHTS RESERVED. NO PART OF THIS BOOK MAY BE REPRODUCED, STORED IN A RETRIEVAL SYSTEM, OR TRANSMITTED IN ANY MEANS, ELECTRONIC, MECHANICAL, PHOTOCOPYING, RECORDING, OR OTHERWISE, WITHOUT THE PERMISSION OF THE PUBLISHER.

DISCLAIMER: THE AUTHOR AND PUBLISHER OF THIS JOURNAL MAKES NO CLAIMS THAT THE CONTENTS OF THIS BOOK CAN OR SHOULD TAKE THE PLACE OF THERAPY FROM A LICENSED PROFESSIONAL IF NEEDED. THE JOURNAL IS INTENDED FOR ENTERTAINMENT PURPOSES ONLY AND SHOULD BE REGARDED AS SUCH. IT IS THE RESPONSIBILITY OF THE JOURNAL OWNER TO MAKE THAT DETERMINATION IF ANY AND ACT RESPONSIBLY. WITH THAT SAID, MAY YOU ENJOY THIS ADULT JOURNAL FOR THE SOUL. - WINDSURF PUBLISHING LLC

About This Journal: A Continuum of Words of Fucking Wisdom A Journal for the Spirited Soul

Let's continue from where we left off with all new fun content! It's really simple. Sometimes we get disappointed or pissed off at people or life situations, and rightfully so. Thus, this journal is a place to give you an opportunity to let out your emotions from feeling afraid, belittled, taken, slighted, and treated badly by others. It's an opportunity to vent, to get things off your chest, let go of past anger, frustration, and any fucking unhappiness. It's also a place to think of the happiness you do have and what you can look forward to in life. It's to help you think about your inner thoughts and situations, feeling yourself fully, and reflect on what has happened to you. Perhaps this will help you happily grow and know yourself all the better to move forward with. It may make you laugh or cry. Yet, its all geared to help you take yourself and your power back. So sit still and write all about you. Let everything hang out freely and feel the emotions that they bring. Embrace them and get to know yourself better. Get more positive with your dreams. Think of how you can have a greater life with new awareness, beginnings, or endings. You deserve a happy life and the fuck best! Remember, your thoughts and positivity help you to create the magic in your life. Peace always, Mimi

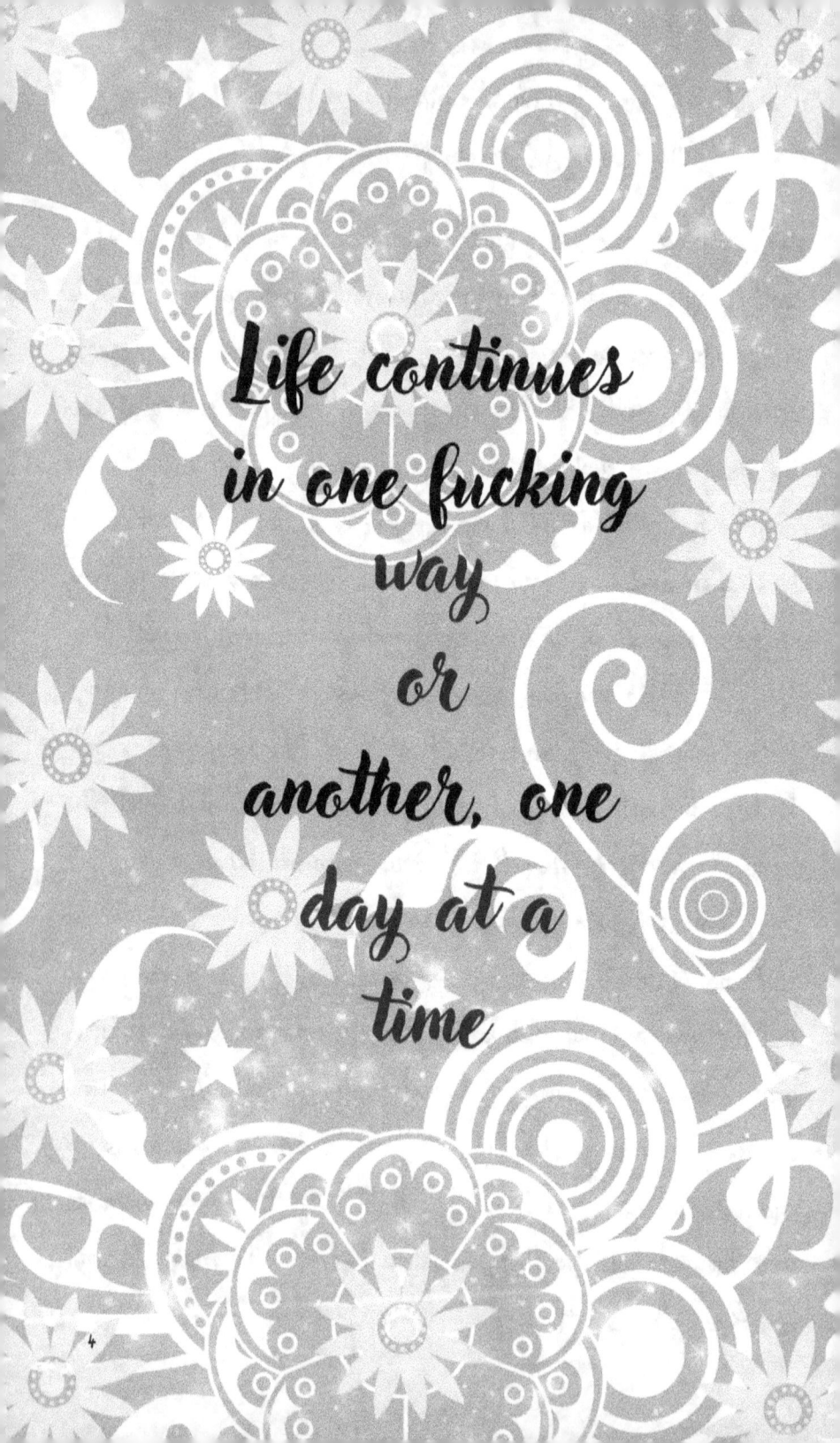

What's new with your life? How have you been redesigning and improving it?

It's always a good time to let go of unnecessary shit

Have you let go of things and thoughts that have held you back lately? Describe some.

Let some light in and fucking joy inside of everyday life

How have you been advancing your overall happiness and joy in life? What are you doing?

Take time to appreciate the fucking brilliance you have within

What are the ways you show self appreciation to yourself? How have you done so lately?

How have you been working at attaining your most personal dreams and goals?

How are you keeping record of your own progress and self development? Describe it.

Always drive yourself to be the best fucking rendition of yourself

Always get out of bad fucking relationships

What bad relationships have you been able to get out of? What happened and how do you feel?

What are you most grateful for lately? Have you recently changed the ways you look at life?

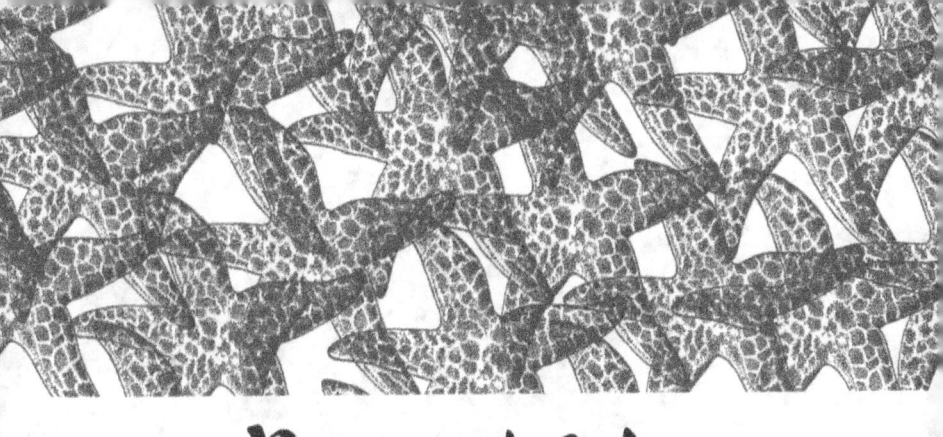

Be grateful
for what you
do have and
what you have
fucking
accomplished

Always give yourself the fucking credit you deserve

What are some things that you deserve credit for? Describe what they are, big and small?

Listen carefully to what your own fucking wisdom is telling you

When you mind is quiet, what are you thinking about? What new wisdom do you have?

How have you connected your thoughts to what you want and what is possible lately? Why?

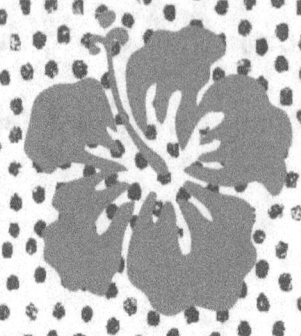

Choices are fucking important when you want change

Make a list of new choices you have or wish to have? Which ones are most important and why?

Always try your fucking hardest to carry your own weight

How have you carried out your own responsibilities in life? Are you satisfied with your decisions and the outcomes? Describe them.

What decisions were or are the most important to you? How did or are you handling them?

Never allow anyone else to make the most fucking important decisions in your life for you

Create a new visual message board for yourself. Describe what's important there. Why?

Use the best fucking visualizations of the future and create a message board for yourself

What makes you feel fulfillment inside? How are your desires connected to this fulfillment?

Contemplate the fulfillment that you fucking desire in your life and why

There are always assholes who will surprise you when you least expect it

Many times people are caught off guard from the assholes of the world. How will you prepare yourself from a sudden attack?

Never fucking agree with an underachiever

How do you handle others who try to impose their own limitations on you? How do you react?

It is important to protect yourself from the fucking harm of people you know

Describe a recent situation you know about when someone wanted to intentionally or unintentionally harm you. What was the outcome?

Protect your possessions from fucking dishonest people

Describe a situation when someone took something materially away from you. What did you do?

Expose the fucking lies of others and set yourself free

What lies have you heard recently? What did you do to free yourself from them?

What life changes are most important to you? What new chances will you give yourself?

There are always going to be some people who are good to you. Write about people who deserve good intentions or deeds from you.

It's always a good idea to be fucking grateful when its due

When was the last time you took a leap of faith?
How did you prepare for the unknown?

Always test the waters fucking carefully before you jump in

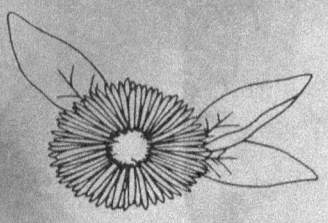

It's most important to focus on the fucking positive in life and expand upon that thinking

How do you get in touch with your own positive thoughts? How do you utilize them in your life?

Raise your glass in peace to others who cheers with you and let them know that they are fucking valued by you

When was the last time you felt ever so happy to be with certain friends and let them know it?

Never let a fucking idiot burst your happy balloons

Think of a happy time when you had to stop the bad behaviors of others. What happened?

What wishes do you have deep in your heart that you hide from others? How will you fulfill them?

If life is like a journey on a highway, you can choose how freely you want to fucking ride it

What choices might you make that can give you more freedom in your life? Describe them.

What does your intuition tell you about yourself, your thoughts, and your own strength?

Your intuitive mind sends you signals and can help you overcome feelings of fucking defeat

What new things can you learn from a class, a special group, or retreat? How can this help you?

There is always something to learn from something and nothing to learn from fucking nothing

Allow good people to help you when you fucking need it

What are things that you can get help with? Who can you go to? What would you say?

Having compassion is a wonderful fucking quality of the spirit and soul

What are ways you can show compassion to others? To yourself? Why is this a good thing?

Be brave on the life journey you are on and keep your fucking chin up when times are hard

Remember times that were the hardest that you got through. Write some things about them.

Believing in miracles is like believing in the magic of life that can redirect fucking destiny

How do you feel about miracles? Do you believe in them and that life can be magical?

People who are shortsighted cut off the flow of fucking possibilities in their lives

Think of a time when you felt completely in a healthy flow of life's possibilities. Describe it.

How can you give of yourself to others? What can you do to make this world a better place?

Giving to others is like fucking giving to yourself

Inner peace is when you know that all is good and you are not bothered by fucking anything anymore

Describe times when you felt the most inner peace? What makes/made you feel this way?

When were times that you felt good karma in your life? What were the circumstances? Describe.

Good karma will always come fucking back

The best people will always want the fucking best for you

How can you tell when the intentions of others are good for you? What are the signs? Describe.

You can learn a lot by what you fucking wanted to be when you were a child

What did you wish to be when you were a child? Has this changed? If so, why has it changed?

People you love or hate make imprints on your mind, spirit, and fucking soul

What memories are most vivid of people who either lifted your mind, spirit, and soul or not?

What memories are most important to you and why? What are the best and the worst?

Thankfully there are always going to be people who you fucking admire and that you look up to

Who are people that you admire and why? What qualities do they have that you like?

There's always some influence that has moved your emotions, triggered your soul, or rocked your fucking spirit

What relationships in your life gives/gave you the most joy and satisfaction? Describe the feeling.

Are you happy with your work? Or, do you dread it? What else would you be doing and why?

It's productive to believe that the best fucking job you can imagine is waiting for you right now

There will always be people who you will not appreciate, like, and might even fucking despise in life

When you're feeling down about how someone is treating you, what can you do to make it better?

There is always someone who loves you and is fucking kindhearted to help you in your life

What is the nicest thing someone has ever done for you? How did you show your gratitude?

Healthy people have good feelings and regards for others, a connection of fucking belonging, kindness, kinship, and heart

What is the kindest thing you have ever done for another person and why? How did this feel?

When you value others, you want them to feel just as fuck good as yourself

What are ways that you add to other peoples well-being and make them feel valued? Explain.

What is the most fun you ever had in your life?
How can you keep some fun always happening?

Everyone gets a taste of fun in life and what a difference it can make to one's fucking sense of happiness

It's wise to let people know how much you love them, as time fucking flies by quickly in life

When was the last time you told someone you loved them? Who were they? What happened?

Everyone has habits that need to change and negativity that needs to be fucking extinguished

What bad habits or negativity can you get rid of? Make a list of what you will do and why.

There's no person who doesn't have some sort of fucking challenges or frustrations

What are your biggest challenges or frustrations? Describe how you will manage them.

There will always be something that will inspire the happy fuck in you and others

When you need inspiration, where or how do you find it? Is what you do effective or not? Why?

There's always a place in the world where you would be so fucking happy to be

Imagine you are any person you wish in any place in the world. What is that place like? What are you doing there? And how do you feel inside?

Everybody has some kind of mantra or mottos about the fucking wisdom of their lives

What are your favorite mottos in life? Write them out. Do you really live them? If no, why?

It's always good to take inventory on your home and how it can change for the fuck better

What does your ideal home look like? How does your home compare? What would you change?

How can you help to make this a better world?
What will you do now and in the future?

ABOUT THE AUTHOR

Mimi Margarita is a created name. Mimi has formal education in art, life coaching, psychology, special needs, writing, and more. She lives in Connecticut and spends her time between Greenwich and New York. Be sure to look for her other books and journals as they become available worldwide.

Additionally, please be kind and take the time to leave a review from where you found this book. Much appreciated. Thank you. Gracias. Merci.